Mapping Global Issues

Immigrants and Refugees

Cath Senker

W
FRANKLIN WATTS
LONDON · SYDNEY

First published in 2011 by Franklin Watts
Copyright © 2011 Arcturus Publishing Limited

Franklin Watts
338 Euston Road
London NW1 3BH

Franklin Watts Australia
Level 17/207 Kent Street, Sydney, NSW 2000

Produced by Arcturus Publishing Limited, 26/27 Bickels Yard, 151–153 Bermondsey Street, London SE1 3HA

The right of Cath Senker to be identified as the author of this work has been asserted by her in accordance with the Copyright, Designs and Patents Act 1988.

Series concept: Alex Woolf   Editor and picture researcher: Alex Woolf
Designer: Jane Hawkins   Map illustrator: Stefan Chabluk

Picture credits: Corbis: 7 (Ricki Rosen), 14–15 (Mike Hutchings/Reuters), 19 (Sophie Elbaz/Sygma), 22–23 (Sukree Sukplang/X90021/Reuters), 27 (Richard Baker/In Pictures), 30–31 (Andrew Lichtenstein), 35 (David Turnley), 39 (Andrea Comas/Reuters), 41 (Andrew Holbrooke), 43 (Shannon Stapleton/Reuters). Shutterstock: 11 (Sam DCruz).

Every attempt has been made to clear copyright. Should there be any inadvertent omission, please apply to the publisher for rectification.

Cover picture: These African migrants are near the Short-Stay Immigration Centre in Melilla, Morocco, waiting to find out whether they will be granted permission to go to Spain, or will be sent back home.

The author would like to acknowledge the following main sources: '2009 Global Trends: Refugees, Asylum-Seekers, Returnees, Internally Displaced and Stateless Persons' (UNHCR, 2010). The Age of Migration by Stephen Castles and Mark J Miller (Palgrave MacMillan, 2009) Human Development Report 2009 (UNDP, 2009). Immigrants: Your Country Needs Them by Philippe Le Grain (Abacus, 2007). No-Nonsense Guide to International Migration by Peter Stalker (New Internationalist, 2008)

Map sources: 9: The Age of Migration: International Population Movements in the Modern World by Stephen Castles and Mark J Miller (Palgrave Macmillan, 2009); 13: UNHCR (2008) and IDMC (2008); 17: de Haas, Hein (2007). The Myth of Invasion: Irregular Migration from West Africa to the Maghreb and the European Union. International Migration Institute, University of Oxford; 21: The Age of Migration: International Population Movements in the Modern World by Stephen Castles and Mark J Miller (Palgrave Macmillan, 2009); 24: Based on figures from report 'Migration in the Asia-Pacific Region' by Graeme Hugo (GCIM, 2005); 29: The Age of Migration: International Population Movements in the Modern World by Stephen Castles and Mark J Miller (Palgrave Macmillan, 2009); 33: HDR team data based on Ratha and Shaw (2006) and World Bank (2009b); 37: Based on figures in 'Population of Foreign Citizens in the EU27 in 2008' (Eurostat, 2009).

A CIP catalogue record for this book is available from the British Library.

Dewey Decimal Classification Number: 305.9'06912

ISBN 978 1 4451 0518 5
SL001634EN
Supplier 03, Date 0911, Print Run 1037

Printed in China

Franklin Watts is a division of Hachette Children's Books, an Hachette UK company.
www.hachette.co.uk

Contents

1: People on the Move   6

2: Sub-Saharan Africa   10

3: The Middle East and North Africa   16

4: The Asia-Pacific Region   20

5: The Americas   28

6: Europe   34

7: The Outlook for the Future   40

Glossary   44

Further Information   45

Index   46

1: People on the Move

Throughout history, people have migrated. This book explores the issue of migration in each continent, looking at why people migrate, where they go and the positive and negative effects on the home and host countries. We will focus on migration between countries, although it is worth remembering that most migrants move within the borders of their own country. In 2009, around 200 million people lived outside their country of birth. They represented just 3 per cent of the world's population.

Migration in recent history

During the 19th century, a huge shift in population occurred. Fifty to sixty million people left Europe between 1800 and 1925 to seek new lives. The majority settled in North America, Australia, New Zealand and Argentina. After World War II (1939–45), it was not just Europeans who were on the move. Asians, Africans and Latin Americans migrated to the developed countries of the West. Since the 1980s, the process of globalization has widened the gap between rich and poor countries, leading to a mushrooming of migration to the wealthier nations.

Who migrates?

It is hardest for the poorest to move, even though they have the greatest reason to do so. They cannot save up enough money to travel and establish themselves in another land. People in the richest countries have the least need to move. Therefore, emigration is lower in the poorest and wealthiest countries than in those with moderate levels of development.

Wherever they come from, most international migrants are enterprising, adventurous people of working age; 45 per cent are women. There are different categories. Permanent settlers, or immigrants, leave their country for good. Many others move temporarily rather than becoming immigrants. Temporary workers enter a country to do a particular job and then return home. Irregular workers enter a country illegally and remain hidden from the authorities. People may change from one category to another. Sometimes, students overstay their visa and become irregular migrants, while irregular migrants might gain permission to stay in a country.

Forced migration

Rather than choosing to move, some people are forced to migrate. Refugees have to escape from their country because of war or persecution. In 2009 there were 14 million refugees worldwide, accounting for about 7 per cent of international migration. An even larger number – around 26 million – have had to abandon their homes and move to another part of their country. They are known as internally displaced persons (IDPs).

PERSPECTIVES

MIGRATION

Migration is the oldest action against poverty. It selects those who most want help. It is good for the country to which they go; it helps break the equilibrium [balance] of poverty in the country from which they come. What is the perversity [unreasonableness] in the human soul that causes people to resist so obvious a good?

Canadian-born US economist
J K Galbraith, 1979

Others are coerced into migrating by human traffickers. For example, in southern Vietnam, some parents are in such desperate poverty that they accept small payments in return for their daughters, who are then sold to brothels over the border in Cambodia.

Where do migrants go and why?

The rise in income inequality between developed and developing countries has made it more worthwhile to migrate from poor to rich countries. In addition, a decrease in the cost of transport and communications has made it easier and cheaper to migrate. Most people move to a country in a similar category of development but with better living standards, although 35 per cent of migration is from developing to developed countries. Even though migrants do not earn as much on average as local people, they will earn a lot more than they would at home.

The majority of migrants select a place where they have contacts already – perhaps they have a relative living in another country or there is a community from their homeland there. Migrants tend to cluster in the same geographical area and do the same type of job. This is often because friends or relatives in the host country introduce them to employers.

A controversial issue

Although the number of migrants from poor to rich countries has increased, migrants still form a small proportion of the population in those lands. Between 1960 and 2010, the share of migrants in developed countries rose from 5 per cent to more than 12 per cent. In the rest of the world, the proportion of foreign-born people is stable or decreasing. Nevertheless, migration causes great controversy, particularly in developed countries. While developing countries often have temporary schemes to permit the entry of low-skilled workers, developed countries tend to be more restrictive. They limit the number of migrants through immigration policies that favour skilled workers but bar low-skilled workers. Yet there is plenty of work available for unskilled migrants.

FACTS and FIGURES

WAGE GAPS BETWEEN NEIGHBOURING COUNTRIES

- The average factory worker in the United States earns four times as much as a Mexican factory worker and 30 times more than a Mexican agricultural worker.

- An unskilled worker in Malaysia makes US$100 a month at home but can earn US$600 a month in Singapore.

- A Polish factory worker takes home US$250 a month but can make US$800 to US$900 a month picking asparagus in Germany.

Source: World Health Organization

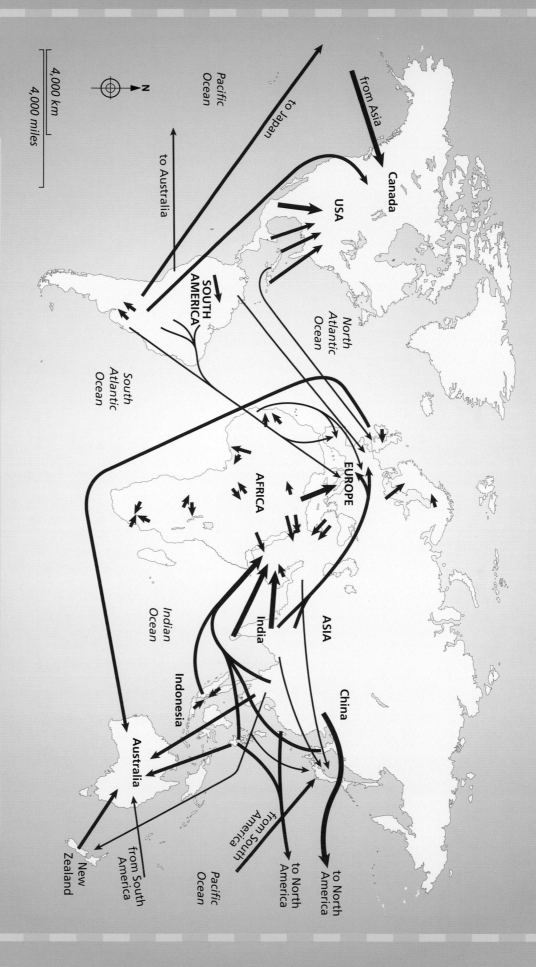

This map shows the main movement of migrants around the world since 1973. The thickness of the arrows gives a rough indication of the numbers who have moved.

4,000 km
4,000 miles

N

from Asia

Canada

Pacific Ocean

to Japan

USA

to Australia

North Atlantic Ocean

SOUTH AMERICA

South Atlantic Ocean

EUROPE

AFRICA

ASIA

India

China

Indian Ocean

Indonesia

from South America

Pacific Ocean

from South America

to North America

to North America

Australia

New Zealand

2: Sub-Saharan Africa

The majority of African migrants go to a neighbouring land. Some migrate further afield, sometimes to the country that used to rule their land as a colony. Others head for the European nations closest to Africa. Many Africans have been forced to flee from conflict or economic crisis. This chapter looks at migration within and from sub-Saharan Africa (the area of the continent south of the Sahara).

Moving for money

Most Africans migrate to improve their opportunities. The economic situation has caused a decline in income for many Africans, while also making it easier to leave. Since the 1980s, international organizations such as the World Bank have told African governments that if they wanted to borrow any more money, they first had to cut spending on health, education and administration. This has reduced the number of skilled jobs in these areas for educated people. Meanwhile, cheaper transport and communications have made it more straightforward for people with money to travel.

However, most African countries are extremely poor. In 2010, 33 of the world's 49 least developed countries were in Africa. The majority of their inhabitants simply cannot afford to move abroad. Relatively few Africans – just 3 per cent – live outside the country of their birth.

Forced out

Millions of Africans living outside their home country did not choose to go but fled as refugees from conflict. For example, Somalia in East Africa has lacked a central government since 1991 and has experienced periodic fighting between rival groups for 20 years. In central Africa, the Democratic Republic of Congo (DRC) suffered a devastating war from 1998 to 2003. Around 4 million people lost their lives, and fighting continues in the eastern region. Thirteen per cent of international migrants in Africa move because of conflict – a larger proportion than in any other continent.

Some people leave to escape both conflict and economic problems. For example, Zimbabwe suffers from a lack of political freedom, an economy in ruins and high unemployment. Yet the government evicts people from their homes to prevent informal (unofficial) trading and makes it extremely hard for them to make a living.

MIXED REASONS FOR MIGRATION

A 42-year-old small trader, a widow with three children, tells her story:

When they destroyed my cottage and stopped us from working I had no money for food or rent or school fees. We slept under the sky in a riverbed for two weeks and my children all became sick and hungry. We went to live with my mother in the rural areas for three months. There was no work and almost no food. We only ate porridge and a little sadza [cooked corn meal].... I left my children and tried for three weeks to sell vegetables ... but the police stopped me.... I came to South Africa in July 2006 to find food for my children.

From 'Neighbors in Need'
(Human Rights Watch, 18 June 2008)

Refugees from DRC cross into Uganda in 2008. They have left home with just the clothes on their backs and a few possessions.

Where do economic migrants go?

Most African migrants head for a nearby country with economic growth and a higher standard of living. They go to Libya, Ivory Coast, Ghana and Gabon in the west, and South Africa and Botswana in the south. West Africa is seen as the most mobile part of Africa. There are major movements from northern inland areas to southern coastal regions. Migrants move to take jobs in factories, mines and plantations (large farms producing crops) or to work in the service sectors of large cities, such as Lagos in Nigeria and Dakar, Senegal. An increasing number of West Africans go further afield, to Libya, South Africa and Botswana. Some migrate to Europe or North America, or even to Japan or China.

South Africa, the wealthiest country of the continent, is hugely attractive to economic migrants. Since the 1990s, migrants from as far away as Ghana, Nigeria and DRC have entered the country. Some well-qualified skilled workers and professionals have found employment in the formal sector (the official economy, in which people pay tax on their income) while others have joined the ever-expanding informal sector – usually working for cash and not paying tax.

Former colonial ties also influence where migrants go. It is easier for people to move to a country that has a link to their own. They usually speak the language of the colonial land. For instance, Belgium ruled DRC from 1885 to 1960. Since DRC became independent, some Congolese have migrated to Belgium; a 2010 survey shows that 40,000 are settled there. Similarly, Senegalese migrants have moved to France and Nigerians to the UK.

Increasingly, irregular African migrants are arriving in European countries with no colonial connections but which are geographically close to Africa, especially Spain, the Canary Islands, Italy and Malta (see Chapter 6). Although there is great alarm in Europe about these arrivals, fewer than 1 per cent of Africans live in Europe.

Where do refugees go?

Refugees usually have little choice but to head for the closest neighbouring country. Political unrest in Zimbabwe has caused millions to flee, the majority to South Africa. Often, African countries in turmoil themselves receive refugees from elsewhere. In 2003 conflict erupted in Darfur, western Sudan, displacing 2 million people from their homes and causing a mass exodus of refugees. In 2010, a quarter of a million Sudanese were sheltering in neighbouring Chad. Yet Sudan itself hosted more than 220,000 refugees from Eritrea, Chad, DRC and other countries. Likewise, in the same year, Ethiopia – which has endured conflict for decades and is one of the world's poorest countries – was sheltering tens of thousands of Somali, Eritrean and Sudanese refugees.

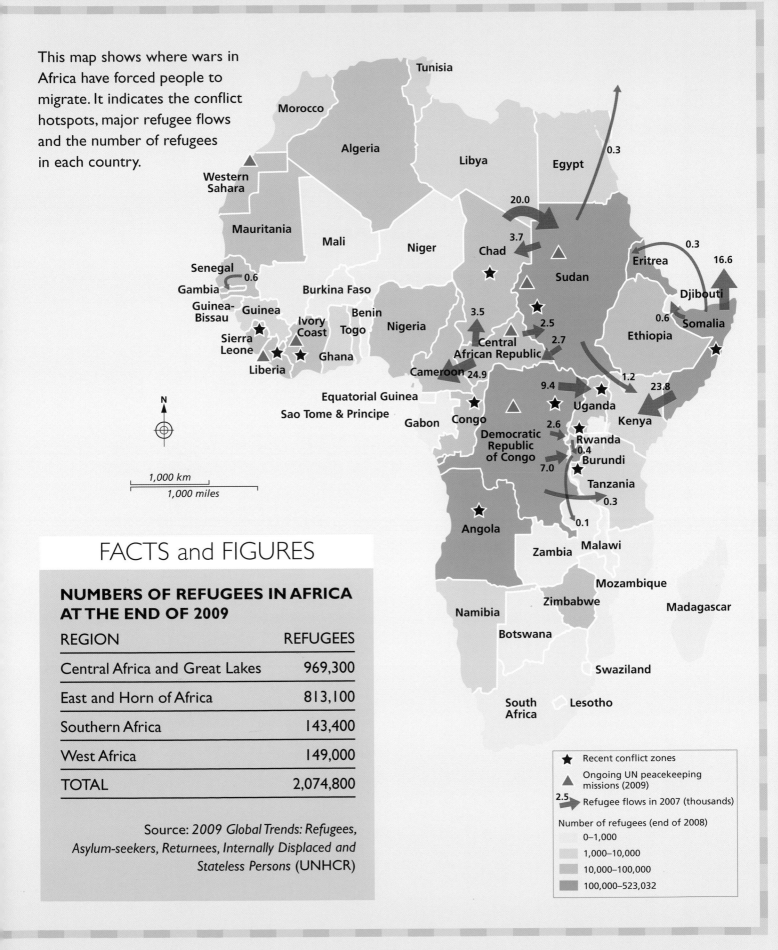

This map shows where wars in Africa have forced people to migrate. It indicates the conflict hotspots, major refugee flows and the number of refugees in each country.

Tunisia

Morocco

Algeria

Libya

Egypt

0.3

Western Sahara

Mauritania

Mali

Niger

20.0

Chad

3.7

0.3

Eritrea

16.6

Senegal

0.6

Sudan

Djibouti

Gambia

Burkina Faso

0.6

Guinea-Bissau

Guinea

Benin

3.5

2.5

Ethiopia

Somalia

Sierra Leone

Ivory Coast

Togo

Nigeria

2.7

Liberia

Ghana

Central African Republic

1.2

23.8

Cameroon

24.9

N

Equatorial Guinea

9.4

Uganda

Kenya

Sao Tome & Principe

Gabon

Congo

2.6

Rwanda

1,000 km

Democratic Republic of Congo

0.4

Burundi

1,000 miles

7.0

Tanzania

0.3

0.1

Angola

Malawi

Zambia

Mozambique

Zimbabwe

Madagascar

Namibia

Botswana

Swaziland

South Africa

Lesotho

FACTS and FIGURES

NUMBERS OF REFUGEES IN AFRICA AT THE END OF 2009

REGION	REFUGEES
Central Africa and Great Lakes	969,300
East and Horn of Africa	813,100
Southern Africa	143,400
West Africa	149,000
TOTAL	2,074,800

Source: *2009 Global Trends: Refugees, Asylum-seekers, Returnees, Internally Displaced and Stateless Persons* (UNHCR)

★ Recent conflict zones

▲ Ongoing UN peacekeeping missions (2009)

2.5 Refugee flows in 2007 (thousands)

Number of refugees (end of 2008)

0–1,000

1,000–10,000

10,000–100,000

100,000–523,032

How does migration affect home countries?

Migration is often necessary, but it does have some negative effects. In Lesotho, around half of all married women have been left for long periods without their husband. Some men leave for up to 15 years to work in South Africa. Their children may grow up without knowing their father.

The 'brain drain' – when skilled and educated people in developing countries migrate and offer their talents elsewhere – is a significant problem, too. It is an especially serious issue in health care because so many African doctors and nurses move to developed countries. A 2005 report showed that there were more Malawian doctors practising in Manchester, UK, than in Malawi! African countries have a huge demand for health care, especially because of the deadly condition, AIDS. In 2008, 1.4 million people across the continent died from AIDS, while another 1.9 million became infected with the virus (HIV) that causes it. Emigration has aggravated the dire shortage of health workers in Africa.

Helping people back home

Migration brings huge benefits, too. Remittances – money sent home by

Patients wait in a long queue for treatment by overworked medical staff at a rural clinic near Lusikisiki in the Eastern Cape, South Africa. Doctors receive good training in South Africa and many migrate for better jobs abroad.

migrants to their families – provide an important source of income. According to the World Bank, migrants sent back US$10.8 billion to Africa in 2007. At first, families spend the extra money on food and household basics. They improve their housing, invest in their children's education and may buy land. Migrants also contribute to community projects back home. For instance, Somali refugees in Minnesota, United States, often take on several jobs to make money. The local Somali coffee shops collect cash from customers and send it via the mosque to their communities surviving in refugee camps in Kenya.

What happens in host countries?

In host countries, the effects are mixed. When large numbers of migrants arrive within a short space of time, tensions can arise. In South Africa, hostility between local people and Zimbabweans resulted in a horrific outbreak of violence in 2008. Mobs hunted down immigrants and raped, robbed and murdered them. On the other hand, immigrants do the low-paid manual jobs that local people often do not want to do. In South Africa, migrants from Lesotho, Mozambique and Swaziland work in the mines. Malawians and Zimbabweans labour as gardeners, while Malawians and Swazi are domestic workers. Wherever they go, African migrants find a niche in the local economy.

3: The Middle East and North Africa

The Middle East and North Africa (MENA) region stretches from Morocco in the west to the western border of Pakistan in the east. Most countries are Arab states, but the area also includes Iran, Turkey and Israel. Many MENA countries have the Muslim religion and culture in common, which aids migration within the region.

Migration within MENA includes the traditional movement of nomadic people and Muslim pilgrims going to Mecca; labour migration, either temporary or permanent; and refugees. This chapter examines migration within, to and from MENA.

Israel, the sole Jewish state, encourages Jewish immigrants, but since there are not enough for its economic needs, it relies on migrants from Romania, the Philippines and Thailand. They come to this developed country to improve their living standards.

Migrating within MENA

The majority of migrants move for economic reasons. The Gulf States – Bahrain, Saudi Arabia, Oman, Kuwait, Qatar and the United Arab Emirates (UAE) – are wealthy countries with extensive oil resources and strong economies. They attract many temporary migrants from Egypt, the Palestinian West Bank and Gaza Strip, Syria and Jordan – places where there are not enough jobs for most of the young people in the population. In Qatar, immigrants make up an astounding 80 per cent of the population, and in the UAE, 70 per cent. As well as Middle Eastern workers, there are large numbers of migrants from South and South-East Asia in the Gulf States (see Chapter 4).

FACTS and FIGURES

REFUGEES IN THE MIDDLE EAST

In 2009, 19 per cent of the world's refugees were in the MENA region. They were mostly Iraqi.

Syria: 1.05 million Iraqi refugees. Syria was the second largest hosting country in the world, after Pakistan.

Iran: 1,070,500 refugees, almost all Afghans

Jordan: 450,800 Iraqi refugees

2009 Global Trends: Refugees, Asylum-seekers, Returnees, Internally Displaced and Stateless Persons (UNHCR)

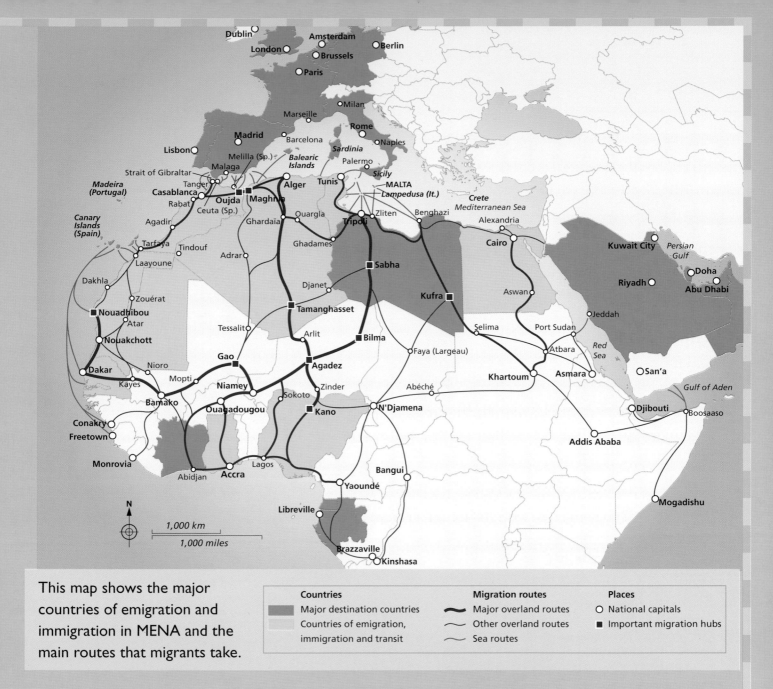

This map shows the major countries of emigration and immigration in MENA and the main routes that migrants take.

Countries
- Major destination countries
- Countries of emigration, immigration and transit

Migration routes
- Major overland routes
- Other overland routes
- Sea routes

Places
- ○ National capitals
- ■ Important migration hubs

Waves of refugees

The existence of Israel in the middle of the Arab world is one of the reasons for political instability in the region that has led to people fleeing as refugees. Israel's establishment in 1948 caused the flight of 750,000 Palestinians. Most of their 4.8 million descendants (their children and grandchildren) still live in MENA, with little hope of returning to Israel/Palestine. Palestinians continue to leave the West Bank and Gaza Strip, because of terrible economic conditions as well as the failure of the peace process with Israel.

Iraqis have been leaving their country in droves since the Gulf War of 1991. A second wave of refugees fled after the US-led invasion of 2003. In 2009 there were

1.8 million Iraqi refugees, mostly sheltering in Syria and Jordan. In that year, Iran hosted 1.1 million refugees, virtually all from Afghanistan, a country that has suffered invasion, occupation and political instability for decades. Also, refugees from countries such as Ethiopia and Eritrea have found their way to nearby MENA countries such as Yemen. Overall, MENA hosted almost a fifth of the world's refugees in 2009.

Emigration outside the region

Middle Eastern people also move outside MENA, especially to Europe, which is the closest developed region and can be reached without air travel. Connections have flourished between particular countries. Turks have been migrating to Germany since they were invited there as 'guest workers' in the 1970s. Moroccans, Algerians and Tunisians have sought work in France, which used to rule their countries as colonies.

Sub-Saharan migrants pass through the MENA countries of Morocco, Libya and Egypt to try to reach Europe. This is called transit migration. Some Africans do manage to enter Europe (see Chapter 6), but large numbers find it impossible because of strict immigration rules. They end up staying in a MENA country, and the transit country becomes their destination.

Migration: negative or positive?

Migration in MENA has various effects. On the negative side, some migrants

CASE STUDY

ASIAN MAID ILL-TREATED

Indonesian maid Sariti Haiti said she was abused and attacked by her Saudi sponsor. A month after she arrived in Saudi Arabia in August 2009, the woman sponsor started to mistreat her. If she was slow to finish her work, the sponsor threw her food in the bin. Then she accused Sariti of stealing her gold. She made her stand in front of the sponsor's sons and removed her clothes to see if she was hiding the gold under her clothes. One day the sponsor beat her over the head with a frying pan. Terrified that her sponsor might kill her, Sariti jumped from the third floor of the apartment building to escape, ending up in hospital with serious injuries.

From 'Indonesian Maid Abuse – Another Saudi Arabian Torture Case Exposed!' by Muhammad Al-Sulami (*Arab News*, February 2010)

suffer poor treatment in the Gulf States, especially Asian workers. An employer has to sponsor them – to agree to employ them for a specific job. Some unscrupulous sponsors abuse the system, for example by confiscating workers' passports to prevent them from changing jobs. Others may even ill-treat their employees.

Refugees also suffer hardship. For instance, Syria and Jordan, both developing countries, have been generous in admitting Iraqi refugees. Yet the high numbers and a shortage of international aid have caused

These two young Filipino women were working in the Gulf state of Kuwait. They escaped the violence and sexual advances of their employers and sought refuge at their country's embassy.

economic strain and led the Syrian and Jordanian governments to restrict refugees' rights. In Syria, Iraqi refugees have access to health care and education but cannot work legally. In Jordan, the majority of refugees have neither the right to work nor to use schools and hospitals. From 2006, Jordan closed its border to most Iraqi refugees.

Overall though, migration has positive effects. MENA countries welcome emigration as a solution to unemployment and a source of remittances, which are particularly important to the economies

of Morocco, Tunisia and Algeria. The host countries also benefit. States such as Qatar and the UAE could not function without migrant labour. A United Nations Development Programme (UNDP) report in 2009 stated that 'migrants boost economic output, at little or no cost to locals'.

4: The Asia-Pacific Region

Asia is a continent on the move – migration within Asia accounts for nearly one-fifth of all migration worldwide. Asian governments welcome temporary migration, although they do not generally allow permanent settlement. People choose to move within the region, to jobs in the Gulf States or to Western countries. Some are forced to leave as refugees.

All kinds of people migrate, from the unskilled to top professionals, including a significant number of women. This chapter looks at migration within, to and from Asia, including Oceania but not the Middle East (see Chapter 3).

Why do people move?

As elsewhere, people migrate to carve out a better life in a richer country. Since the 1990s, the major growth of migration has been within Asia, from the less developed countries to the newly industrializing countries, known as the 'tiger' economies: Singapore, Taiwan, South Korea and Hong Kong. Rapidly industrializing countries need labour for their factories, as well as foreign professionals because their education systems cannot produce skilled people quickly enough. Although Asian countries rarely permit permanent migration, they make an exception for marriage migration. Women from poor backgrounds move to other Asian countries to marry better-off men.

Conversely, Australia and New Zealand encourage permanent migration. Australia

FACTS and FIGURES

ASIAN MIGRANTS

- In the early 21st century, around 6.1 million Asians were employed outside their own countries within the Asian region, while 8.7 million were working in the Middle East.

- In 2005 there were at least 20 million Asian migrant workers worldwide.

- A large proportion of Asian migrants are female. In 2004, 81 per cent of migrants from Indonesia were women, while in 2006, 72 per cent of Filipino migrants were female.

    Source: World Health Organization

attracts many Asian immigrants, as well as workers from Latin America, the countries of the former Soviet Union, the Middle East and South Africa. All legal immigrants have the right to bring their family. In the early 21st century, Australia planned to boost immigration. New Zealand also has a substantial immigrant population, mostly from Asia and the Pacific.

Forced to leave

In 2009 the Asia-Pacific region hosted more than one-third of the world's refugees, three-quarters of them Afghans. Some three decades of conflict in Afghanistan have forced large numbers of refugees to shelter in neighbouring Pakistan and Iran. These two countries host the biggest refugee populations in the world. Asian lands also host refugees from other long-term conflicts in the region, such as those in Tibet, Burma and Sri Lanka. Human trafficking is a particular problem in South-East Asia. An estimated 200,000 to 250,000 women and children are trafficked each year. Most are sold as sex workers.

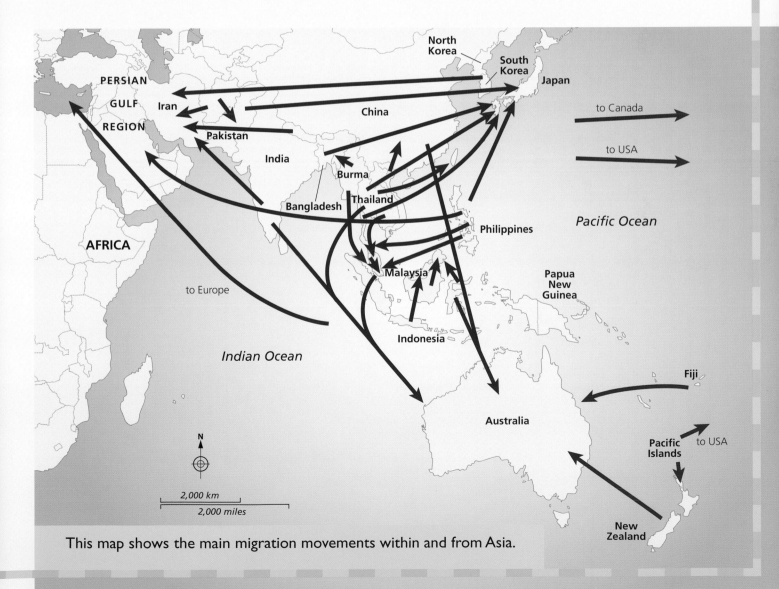

This map shows the main migration movements within and from Asia.

Where do workers go?

All Asian countries have both immigration and emigration, although the balance varies depending on their economic situation. Wealthy countries such as Hong Kong, Japan, Singapore, South Korea and Taiwan are mostly countries of immigration.

The countries mainly of emigration include Bangladesh, Burma, China, India, Indonesia and Pakistan. Malaysia and Thailand have large numbers of both immigrants and emigrants. Despite all this movement, migrants make up a small proportion of the total labour force in many Asian countries – around 4 per cent in East and South-East Asia. In Singapore, however, the figure is 28 per cent, and in Malaysia, 12 per cent.

Jobs in countries with strong economies are at a premium, but would-be migrants may have no connections in their destination country. They may turn to a broker to find a job for them and organize their paperwork and transport, which is extremely expensive. Some migrants to Taiwan pay the vast sum of US$5,000 to

PERSPECTIVES

A CHINESE WOMAN GOES TO SOUTH KOREA TO MARRY

There were many people who went to work in Korea from my hometown. They became richer and built nice houses when they came back.... I was keen to work in Korea. But it was quite difficult to get a working visa. One of my acquaintances introduced me to a Korean man. I just thought that I would marry him and as soon as I arrive[d] in Korea, I would run away from him and work somewhere. But the guy was quite gentle to me. We just fell in love with each other after several meetings.... But you have to know it, most foreign brides come to Korea because of poverty.

From 'Marriage Migrant Women in Korea and Attempts to Organize Them' by Lee Inkyoung

brokers for a job contract. Most people cannot afford the exorbitant fees, so they may take the risk of moving illegally. Irregular migrants make their way from Indonesia and Thailand to Malaysia, while Thailand itself has many irregular workers, especially from Burma.

Where do migrant brides go?

Since the 1990s, more and more women have migrated for marriage. Again, they usually go to a richer country. They journey from the Philippines, China and South Korea to Japan, and from Vietnam and Thailand to Taiwan. In China, farmers seek wives from Vietnam, Laos and Burma, while marriage migration to South Korea is also on the rise. The brides are often young and poorly educated. They have to cope with moving to another country where they do not speak the language and have no friends or family, to marry a person they have never met. These brave young women go to extraordinary lengths to improve their lives.

A migrant from the poor country of Burma works in a garment factory in Thailand. Employers in Thailand often ignore the labour laws and force employees to work long hours.

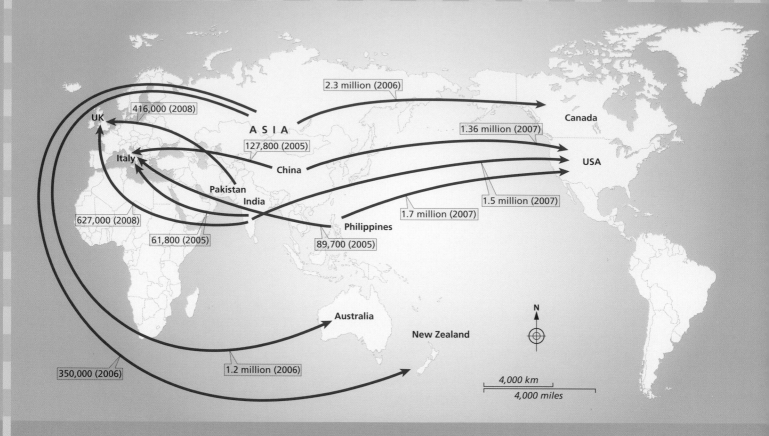

2.3 million (2006)

416,000 (2008)

UK

ASIA

127,800 (2005)

Canada

1.36 million (2007)

Italy

China

USA

Pakistan

India

1.5 million (2007)

627,000 (2008)

Philippines

1.7 million (2007)

61,800 (2005)

89,700 (2005)

Australia

New Zealand

N

350,000 (2006)

1.2 million (2006)

4,000 km
4,000 miles

This map indicates that Asian migrants have journeyed in large numbers across the world, to Europe, North America and Oceania. The United States is the most popular destination country.

Going to the Gulf

Labour migration outside the Asia-Pacific region is also rising. Contract labourers – taken on to do a specific job – travel in their thousands to the oil-rich Gulf States. These countries are short of skilled workers because most local people work in the public sector (the government-run part of the economy).

The private sector (the part of the economy not under government control) depends on foreign labour. In the Gulf States, many foreign workers are low-skilled, but nowadays there are growing numbers of migrants in construction managerial or technical posts.

Long-distance migration

Some Asian migrants depart from the continent altogether, aiming for the United States, Canada, Australia and New Zealand. Since 1992, people of Asian origin have made up around one-third of immigrants to the United States. Family reunion accounts for a large proportion of the immigrants to these countries – people arrive to join families who have already settled abroad. The sources of migrants have become more diverse over the years; in particular, the number of Chinese migrants has risen dramatically.

Who is welcome?

The United States, Canada, Australia and New Zealand encourage skilled and business migrants from Asia. During the 1990s, half of all graduate migrants who arrived in the United States were Asian, the largest numbers coming from India and China. Destination countries also welcome migrants who can care for their rapidly ageing populations. For instance, nurses and caregivers from the Philippines go to the United States and Canada. In recent years, more Asians have started migrating to Europe, especially from China, India, Japan, the Philippines, Vietnam and Thailand. They include medical and IT workers, female domestic workers (in southern Europe particularly) and manual workers.

And who is not?

Skilled workers are welcomed, yet despite the availability of jobs, developed countries restrict the entry of unskilled labourers. Therefore, these workers tend to be irregular migrants. Many go to extreme lengths to try to enter European countries. Some Chinese migrants pay people smugglers to organize their passage across the Pacific, locked in cargo containers on ships. Travellers can pay up to US$60,000 to a smuggler for a trip from Fujian, China, to the United States.

Others choose the UK as their destination – slightly cheaper at US$45,000.

Migrants may pay for this risky mode of passage with their lives. For instance, in June 2000, the bodies of 58 Chinese migrants were discovered in a container in Dover, England. Tragically, they had suffocated to death through lack of oxygen in the container. Despite the dangers, others still attempt to make similar journeys.

CASE STUDY

FROM SHANGHAI TO SEATTLE IN A METAL BOX

Crews removing a container in Seattle, USA, noticed it was lighter than it should have been if it were carrying 20 tonnes of merchandise. A security officer noticed two men and a woman wandering around. Upon searching, guards rounded up a total of 18 men and four women. The stowaways had spent 15 days crossing the Pacific Ocean from Shanghai, China, in a metal cargo container. They had blankets, clothing, water and tools, and fans to disperse the air. Nevertheless, owing to the piles of uneaten food and containers full of human waste, the stench was terrible. The Chinese stowaways, in remarkably good health considering their ordeal, were taken into custody.

From '15 Days in a Metal Box to be Locked Up' by Lornet Turnbull, Kristi Heim, Sara Jean Green and Sanjay Bhatt (*Seattle Times*, April 2006)

What are the effects of migration?

For host countries, the efforts of migrants to reach their shores have several positive effects. Professionals fill vacancies at the top of the job ladder. For example, newly industrializing Singapore has recruited foreign professionals; around 20 per cent of its immigrants are doctors, teachers or other highly skilled people. Immigrants usually fill the gaps at the bottom rung of the employment ladder, too. Female migrants undertake childcare and domestic work, allowing women in the host country to have a career. In South Korea, local people are not keen to undertake manual work, but migrants are prepared to work long hours for low pay in factories. In regions where settlement has been going on for a long time, such as Oceania, evidence shows that immigrants create as many jobs as they occupy.

There are downsides, too. The vast numbers of refugees in Asia have created a challenge for governments, especially in Pakistan and also Iran (see Chapter 3). Pakistan shelters the largest number of refugees in relation to its economic capacity – that is, it bears the heaviest cost when taking into account the size of its economy. Yet forced migration forms just a small proportion of overall migration in the region. There were 3.9 million refugees in Asia at the end of 2009, while the continent hosted 61 million migrants in 2010.

Helpful to the home countries?

As in Africa, the loss of highly qualified Asian migrants has, in some cases, led to a brain drain back home. Home countries sometimes suffer skill shortages and need to attract migrants themselves. Taiwan, for example, is now trying to persuade emigrants to return.

However, in general, countries of emigration see the movement of workers as vital to their economy. Some countries, such as India, have surplus graduates, so emigration helps to reduce unemployment and provides workers with training and experience. Migration helps to reduce poverty, too. For instance, in Andhra

PERSPECTIVES

THE BENEFITS OF SKILLED MIGRATION

Harinder Takhar, Indian migrant to Canada, community leader and Minister of Government Services from 2009, says:

[Skilled migration] gives us access to a pool of talent not otherwise available. Half our engineers are foreign. They went to the very best schools. Thanks to them, productivity and quality are improved. It's a question of drive and sheer hard work. The construction industry in British Columbia is now owned by visible [non-white] immigrants. All taxi drivers and independent truck drivers are immigrants.

From *Immigrants: Your Country Needs Them* by Philippe Le Grain (Abacus, 2007)

Pradesh and Madhya Pradesh in India, the rate of poverty in a house with a migrant fell by about 50 per cent between 2001–2 and 2006–7. A similar effect was found in Bangladesh. Overall, both host and home countries benefit from migration.

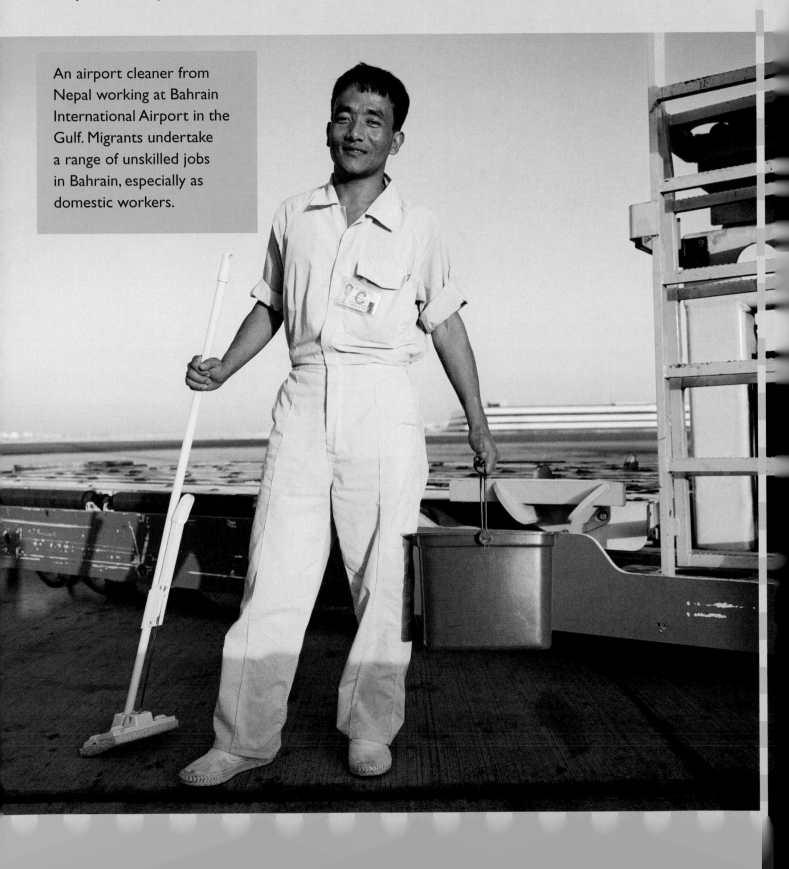

An airport cleaner from Nepal working at Bahrain International Airport in the Gulf. Migrants undertake a range of unskilled jobs in Bahrain, especially as domestic workers.

5: The Americas

The Americas include the developed nations of Canada and the United States and the developing countries of Latin America, including the Caribbean. Migration occurs between Latin American lands, some experiencing both immigration and emigration. Yet the trend is towards more migration to the richer northern American countries, where living standards are higher. This chapter looks at migration within, to and from the Americas.

Why migrate?

Economic globalization has increased the inequality between the rich northern American countries and the poorer nations of Latin America. In Brazil, for example, the average wage in manufacturing in 2005 was US$4.10 an hour. In the United States it was US$23.70 – nearly six times higher! Even working in low-waged jobs in the United States, Brazilians can earn far more than they can at home. Economic crises, such as the one that hit Argentina from 2001 to 2003, have left a legacy of poverty and unemployment, creating a further incentive to migrate.

Being close to a rich country offers another good reason to migrate. Mexico is the poorer neighbour of the United States and provides almost a third of its total immigrants. Mexicans are frequently involved in circular migration. They go to work for a while in the United States and return to spend time in Mexico with their friends and family. Then they re-enter the United States for another period of work. Some migrants from the Dominican Republic in the Caribbean take advantage of their closeness to Puerto Rico. They stay for a while, picking up the local accent and

FACTS and FIGURES

FAMILY REUNIONS

- In 2008, 44.1 per cent of new legal immigrants (lawful permanent residents) to the United States were immediate relatives of a US citizen, while 20.5 per cent were more distant relatives who came with a Family Preference visa.

- In Canada, 22.5 per cent of immigrants in 2008 came under the family reunion programme.

Source: World Health Organization

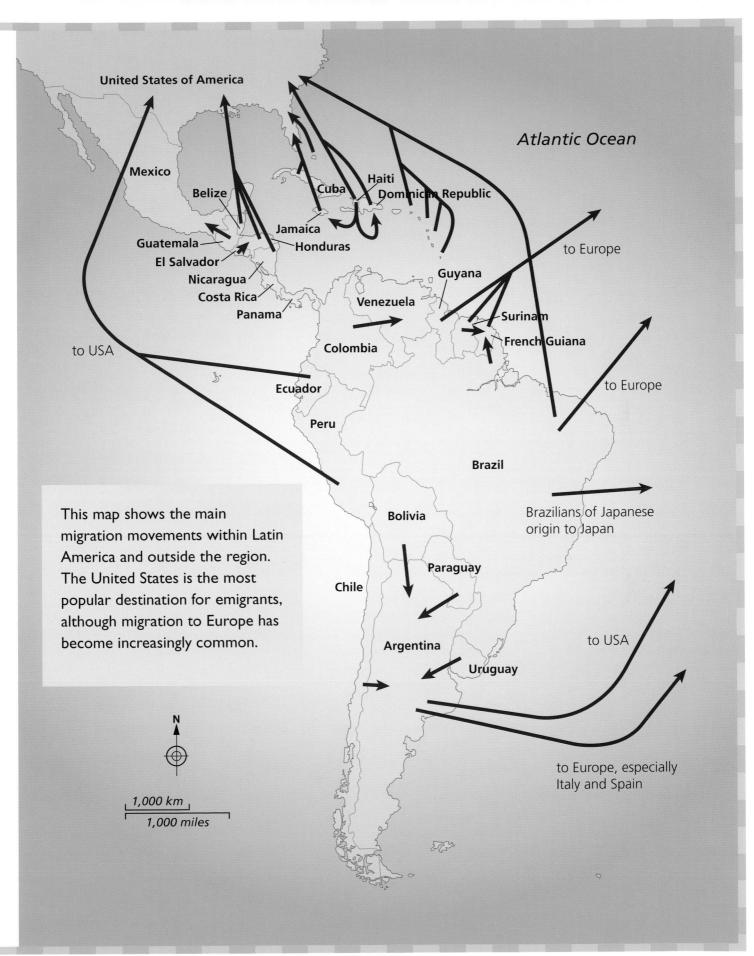

United States of America

Atlantic Ocean

Mexico

Belize

Cuba   Haiti
Dominican Republic

Guatemala
El Salvador   Jamaica   Honduras
Nicaragua
Costa Rica
Panama

to USA

to Europe

Guyana

Venezuela

Surinam

Colombia

French Guiana

Ecuador

Peru

to Europe

This map shows the main migration movements within Latin America and outside the region. The United States is the most popular destination for emigrants, although migration to Europe has become increasingly common.

Brazil

Bolivia

Brazilians of Japanese origin to Japan

Paraguay

Chile

to USA

Argentina

Uruguay

N

1,000 km
1,000 miles

to Europe, especially Italy and Spain

buying false documents so they can pass as Puerto Ricans. Puerto Ricans may freely enter the United States.

Refugees and trafficking

The biggest haven for refugees in the region is the United States, which hosted 275,000 of them in 2009. Refugees from across the globe apply for admission to the country; that year, the greatest numbers came from Iraq and Burma.

Mexicans working in the fields in North Carolina, USA. Such labourers often work on a casual basis; each day they get up early and hope they will be recruited for a job.

CASE STUDY

THE EXTREME RISKS OF MIGRATION

Inmer Omar Rivera, an electrician from Honduras, is desperate to reach the United States. Currently staying in a hostel for migrants in Ciudad Juárez, Mexico, Inmer travelled 2,000 kilometres by train over 20 days to Mexico. Of the 2,000 who boarded the train initially, only 20 arrived. Relying on strangers to give them food, they ate on eight days alone. At military checkpoints, the migrants had to decide whether to jump off the train and wait for the next one or stay on and hide. Inmer was lucky. Sometimes he left the train and soldiers got on; other times, he remained and those who jumped off were caught. Many who jumped off died of their injuries. Having survived this extraordinary journey, Inmer fears being caught and sent back to Honduras.

From *Immigrants: Your Country Needs Them* by Philippe Le Grain (Abacus, 2007)

The other main form of forced migration is people trafficking. In the early 21st century, there was a growing problem of trafficking from Latin America to the United States. A report in 2007 estimated that up to 17,500 people were trafficked to the United States annually, including children. Latin American orphans and street children are vulnerable to trafficking because they often have no adult to watch out for them. They may be taken and sold as sex workers or domestic servants.

Which destination?

Migration within Latin America remains important – for example, from Colombia to oil-rich Venezuela, and from various

countries to Argentina. Argentina is a country of both immigration and emigration. Over 65 per cent of migrants are from other South American countries. However, increasing numbers of Argentinians are moving to the United States and also to Spain and Italy, which have special policies to allow them entry. Brazilians move to Portugal (which ruled Brazil as a colony), the United States or Japan, along with other Latin Americans of Japanese origin.

The United States has experienced an upswing in non-European immigration since 1970, especially from neighbouring Mexico. Even though the United States restricts Mexican immigrants and forcefully polices the border, irregular migrants risk treacherous trips through the desert in an attempt to sneak in. Canada is also a popular destination. It has a policy to admit the equivalent of 1 per cent of its total population each year. Since Canada relaxed its immigration rules in the 1960s, more migrants have arrived there from Asia, Africa and the Middle East, rather than just from Europe as before.

What work do they do?

Migrants' job opportunities depend on their country of origin, whether they are legal or irregular, and their level of skills. In Argentina, for instance, irregular migrants often work in domestic service, construction, textile factories and agriculture.

The United States and Canada both aim to attract professionals. For instance, the United States grants special visas to highly skilled applicants to fill posts for which there is no suitable local candidate. Yet the majority of migrants are in unskilled jobs. Mexicans are heavily employed in agriculture. California produces around one-quarter of the world's strawberries. Strawberries are soft and have to be harvested by hand rather than with machines. Farmers rely on Mexican immigrants for the job. This is known as the 'Mexicanization' of agriculture – as opposed to 'mechanization'. Other migrants become healthcare or construction workers, au pairs, nannies, cleaners or taxi drivers.

How are the host countries affected?

In the United States and Canada, some people claim that immigrants take jobs from local people and cause wages to fall. Evidence from both countries shows that recent immigrants and the lowest-skilled people are the most likely to lose out from immigration. Yet immigrants often set up their own businesses and create job opportunities for local people.

In the United States, great concern exists over irregular migration. Resources have been invested in the attempt to police the US–Mexico border and prevent Mexicans and other Latin Americans from entering the United States. However, employers benefit from the flexible labour offered by irregular migrants. They can offer them less money, employ them when they are needed and lay them off when they are no longer required. The migrants cannot complain about low pay or claim welfare benefits when they are out of work. They are not legally in the country so they have to remain hidden from the authorities. Canada does not experience the same contradictory situation. It has a clearer immigration policy that aims to expand the population.

PERSPECTIVES

WINNERS AND LOSERS

The laws of supply and demand imply that, other things being equal, an increase in the number of low-skilled immigrants will lower the wages of comparable native workers, at least in the short run, because they now face stiffer competition in the labor market. In contrast, high-skilled workers may gain from the influx of immigrant labor. Not only will they pay less for the services these laborers provide, such as painting the house and mowing the lawn, but by hiring immigrant workers they will be able to specialize in producing the goods and services to which their skills are better suited.

George J Borjas, US campaigner against
low-skilled immigration
(*National Review*, April 2006)

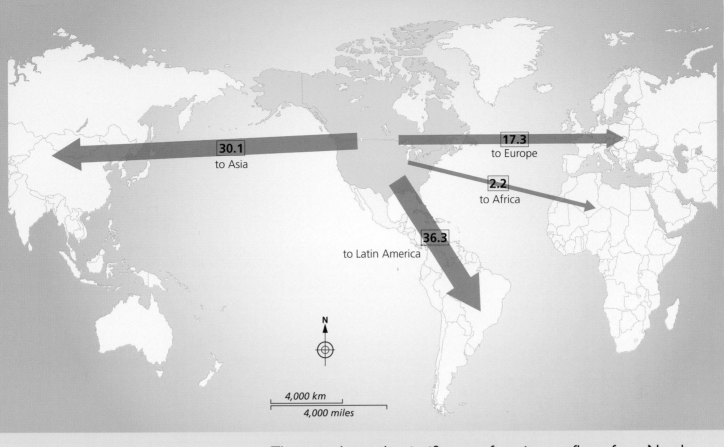

| 2.2 | Remittances, 2006 (in US$ billions) |

This map shows the significance of remittance flows from North America to other regions. The thickness of the arrows indicates the size of the remittances.

What happens in the home countries?

As elsewhere, remittances – mostly from the United States but also from Spain, Canada and Italy – benefit migrants' families and communities in Latin America. They have a 'multiplier effect'. For example, farmers back home use the funds to buy equipment and fertilizers that boost their output. They make more money, invest further and create employment. Mexicans in the United States have 'hometown associations' that support community activities in their home area.

Migrants often return home and establish new businesses; this is common in the Dominican Republic. Yet this can bring disadvantages too. When returning migrants buy up land, this helps their families but may lead to a shortage of land for others. This problem has occurred in the Caribbean.

As in other regions, the brain drain affects the countries of emigration, a particular difficulty for small countries. In 2000 a massive 80 per cent of university-educated people in Guyana, Jamaica and Haiti had left to work in rich countries.

6: Europe

As one of the developed regions of the world, Europe is a magnet for migrants. People come from other continents while Europeans from poorer countries migrate to the wealthier economies. Since the expansion of the European Union (EU) in 2004 and 2007, hundreds of thousands of eastern Europeans have headed for northern Europe. This chapter explains the major patterns of migration within, to and from Europe.

Why migrate to Europe?

The northern European economies are the richest and most attractive to migrants, while the southern regions have also developed strong economies and become countries of immigration. Migrants meet the expanding demand for skilled and low-skilled workers in the service sector, including health care, hotels and catering. They fill posts in the informal sector, doing unofficial, casual jobs that are not taxed or monitored by the government.

In rich, industrial countries, many people are educated and they reject manual work and unskilled jobs. Therefore vacancies abound in low-wage sectors such as agriculture. For example, British farmers rely on fruit and vegetable pickers from eastern Europe. The workers undertake 12-hour shifts, every day of the week, for around US$8 an hour. In developed countries, women with children want to go out to work.

Families need childcare and help with the housework to make this possible. Latin American women, who speak Spanish, can find employment in Spanish households.

Poorly paid skilled jobs with long working hours and stressful conditions, such as nursing, prove unpopular among locals too. Britain's National Health Service relies on migrant staff. Over 60 per cent of nurses and care workers in London in 2007–8 were migrants.

Push factors

There are factors pushing people to migrate, too. After 1989, the former Communist countries of eastern Europe were transformed. Their governments no longer controlled the countries' economies, and people were free to set up businesses. Although new economic opportunities arose, Eastern Europeans were no longer guaranteed a basic level of public housing, education and welfare. This led to greater inequality between those who benefited and those who lost out under the new economic conditions. There was a rise in unemployment, leading more people to consider migration.

People from outside the EU also migrate to take advantage of better economic opportunities. The differences in living standards between non-European and Northern European countries are even starker than the divisions within the continent. Family reunion is another significant factor in migration, accounting for nearly three-fifths of legal immigration to the EU.

FACTS and FIGURES

MIGRATION IN EUROPE

- Most of the population expansion in the EU during the first decade of the 21st century was due to migration.
- 56 per cent of migrants in the EU are citizens of another European country.
- 75 per cent of the EU's migrants live in Germany, Spain, the UK, France and Italy.

Source: Eurostat, 2009

A laundry worker in an immigrant neighbourhood of Paris, France. Although developed countries have growing requirements for skilled workers, many unskilled manual labourers are also required to service society's needs.

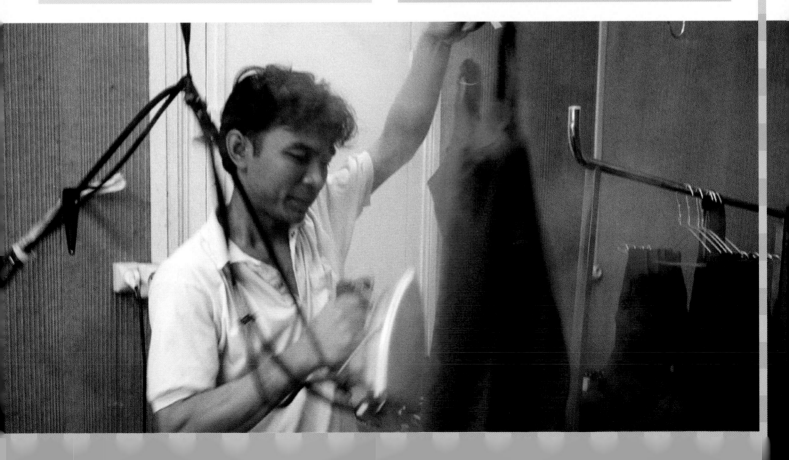

Where do migrants go?

In 2004, the EU was enlarged to include ten mostly eastern European members, and in 2007, Romania and Bulgaria joined the union. In 2004, most of the 15 existing EU states restricted migration from the new member states. However, Ireland, the UK and Sweden opened their doors to migrants. There were major influxes of Poles and people from the Baltic states (Estonia, Latvia and Lithuania) to Ireland and the UK – although not to Sweden, which lacked good job opportunities at the time.

Other countries with many migrants are the wealthy nations of Germany, France and Switzerland. Most migrants in Germany are Turkish, Italian or Polish; those in France are Portuguese, Algerian or Moroccan. In Switzerland, they are mainly European.

In the early 2000s, the southern European nations of Italy, Spain, Portugal and Greece also experienced a rise in migration. Romanians form the largest group in Spain and Italy, while Spain has the largest Latin American population in Europe: over 420,000 Ecuadorians and 280,000 Colombians in 2008.

Irregulars take risks

While some migrants, such as Latin Americans, are allowed to enter Spain and Italy, many other hopeful migrants, particularly from North Africa, have no legal option. They make difficult and dangerous journeys in the attempt to reach Mediterranean Europe illegally, often risking their lives in flimsy boats. For instance, many would-be immigrants attempt the 96-kilometre crossing from North Africa to Lanzarote or Fuerteventura, in the Spanish-owned Canary Islands – a 20-hour rowing trip. Others take a high-speed boat from Albania or Croatia to Italy. Since it is prohibited to transport migrants in this way, drivers may dump passengers overboard if they think they are likely to be caught by Italian customs officials. An estimated 2,000 people a year die crossing the Mediterranean Sea to Europe.

CASE STUDY

SURVIVING MIGRANT LIFE IN THE UK

To achieve the better life they yearn for, migrants often work overtime (extra hours), take on more than one job or frequently switch jobs, seeking higher pay. Mario, from Portugal, started off as a hotel waiter in Eastbourne, worked in a couple of glass and window factories, and later moved to London to work as a cleaner. But the job paid the minimum wage – the lowest legal wage – and the tasks were excessive. He was sacked for taking time off with a bad back. Mario then found work as a security guard, which he felt offered more opportunities. He hoped to progress to become a supervisor and improve his living standards.

From *Global Cities at Work* by Jane Wills, Kavita Datta, Yara Evans, Joanna Herbert, Jon May and Cathy McIlwaine (Pluto, 2010)

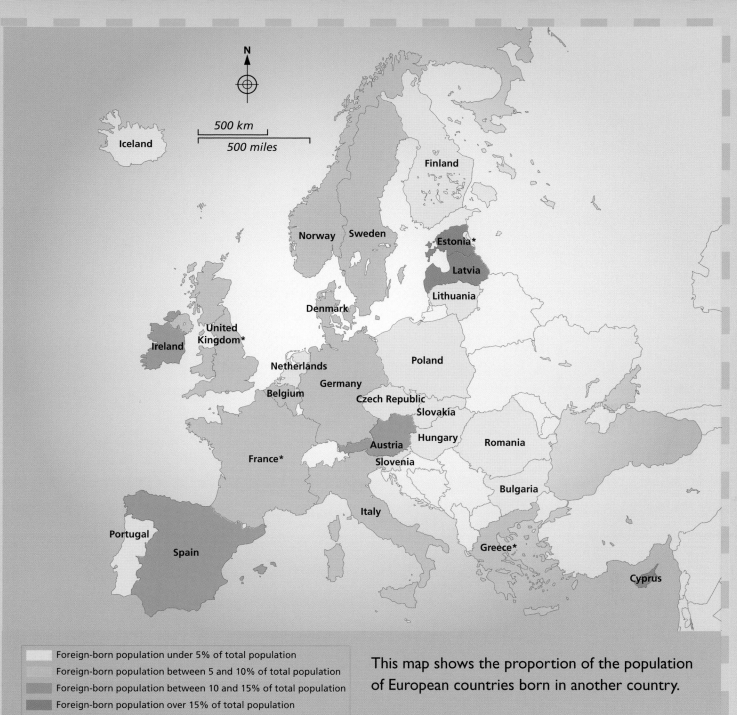

N

500 km
500 miles

Iceland

Finland

Norway   Sweden

Estonia*

Latvia

Lithuania

Denmark

Ireland

United
Kingdom*

Netherlands

Belgium

Germany

Poland

Czech Republic

Slovakia

France*

Austria

Hungary

Romania

Slovenia

Bulgaria

Italy

Portugal

Spain

Greece*

Cyprus

Foreign-born population under 5% of total population
Foreign-born population between 5 and 10% of total population
Foreign-born population between 10 and 15% of total population
Foreign-born population over 15% of total population
* Data for this country has been estimated by Eurostat

This map shows the proportion of the population
of European countries born in another country.

Emigration

While the media focus on immigration –
especially sensational stories of illegal
immigrants – it is worth noting that Europe
has a high level of emigration, too. Foreign
nationals leave and Europeans move to
other countries. In Spain, for instance, the
British formed the fourth largest group of
non-nationals in 2008, while other Britons
favoured France, Australia and New Zealand.

How are home countries affected?

Migrant workers in Europe can earn far higher incomes than at home. For example, wages in Poland are typically one-fifth of those in the UK. Many Poles came to work for a few years during the first decade of the 21st century and then returned home with their savings. A downside was that Poland experienced a loss of skilled personnel, causing labour shortages during those years of mass emigration. As regards non-European migrants from developing countries, wages from even the lowest-paid jobs are sufficient to allow them to send remittances to their families.

What happens in host countries?

Some observers argue that high levels of immigration create difficulties for host societies. Firstly, large numbers of migrants arrive, although many local people are out of work. They say that if immigration stopped, unemployment would go down. Yet evidence from the UK and Ireland after the EU expansion in 2004 counters this argument. The new workers filled vacancies for skilled workers or took low-paid jobs that local people refused to do. There was no increase in unemployment or fall in wages. During the economic downturn in 2008, fewer jobs were available, so fewer migrants opted to move to another country for a job. For instance, the number of eastern European workers registering to work in the UK during the first three months of 2008 was 25 per cent lower than in the third quarter of 2007.

Secondly, there is concern about the number of irregular migrants. Even though governments have tried to restrict the entry of low-skilled migrants, there is still a demand for their labour, so they often come through irregular routes. Spain and Italy have tried to tackle this issue. Although most people arrive illegally or overstay their visas, they are often legalized later – they receive permission to remain in the country. Spain has attempted to work with African

PERSPECTIVES

WE ALL BENEFIT FROM MIGRATION

Peter Stalker is a campaigner against immigration controls. He argues:

[I]n almost all cases migration is good for both source and destination countries. Indeed the world as a whole would be much better off. One estimate suggests that relaxing the movement of temporary workers even at the level of 3 per cent of the labour force of the high-income countries would result in annual global income gains of $150 billion – since they would both boost economic activity in their destination countries and also send money home.

Removing all immigration barriers would thus make the whole world a lot richer.

From *The No-Nonsense Guide to International Migration* by Peter Stalker (New Internationalist, 2008)

countries to reduce numbers making the hazardous journey. For instance, in 2008 Spain signed an agreement with Mali to allow the legal recruitment of workers. Arrangements like this could help to reduce the smuggling of migrants by allowing a legal entry route.

Some sub-Saharan African migrants try to reach Europe by travelling to Ceuta and Melilla, areas of Morocco ruled by Spain. These migrants are near the immigration centre in Melilla, waiting to find out if they can stay or must return home.

7: The Outlook for the Future

A variety of factors will influence migration in the future. Economic circumstances will affect migrants' choice of destination, as will demographic trends and the effects of climate change. The trade rules between countries can make a difference, too. Immigration policies can make it easier or harder for people to migrate.

Economic factors

In general, there will be more internal migration from rural to urban areas, and from developing countries to the developed world. Migrants will still be drawn to the oil-rich states of Saudi Arabia, UAE, Libya and Venezuela.

In terms of regions, economic growth is likely to be strong in the Asia-Pacific region, so migration within the area will probably rise. Greater numbers of migrant workers could have social and political effects. Until now, Asian countries have promoted only temporary migration and resisted allowing migrants to move permanently. This could change as they increasingly depend on migrants to do their 'dirty, dangerous and difficult' (3D) jobs and on professionals to fill gaps where there are skill shortages.

In Latin America, immigration to Canada and the United States will remain popular, while fewer migrants are likely to travel between countries of the region. Immigration to Europe is expected to expand, too. Africans will carry on migrating to wealthier parts of the continent, while greater numbers will probably attempt to reach Europe, whatever the restrictions imposed by European governments.

Demographic trends

Changes in population will affect migration too. Developed countries in particular have rapidly ageing populations. Families are having fewer children while people tend to live longer. This leads to a diminishing number of working people able to support the retired population. For example, it is projected that the working-age population in the EU will fall by 16 per cent between 2004 and 2050, while the proportion of people over 65 will rise by a dramatic 77 per cent. Immigration can help to solve this problem, and is likely to continue.

The world's population is ageing but also rising rapidly. By 2050 it is predicted there will be over 9 billion people on the planet – up from 6.8 billion in 2010.

An Indian construction worker on a building site in Dubai in the United Arab Emirates. The Gulf States are likely to continue to be a magnet for migrant workers.

Where population growth puts pressure on resources, it will force people to migrate.

Climate change

Climate change – the gradual warming of the planet – will exacerbate this problem. Several regions of developing countries will be severely affected. For instance, parts of southern Africa are becoming drier, leading to increasing droughts – dry periods with little rain. In contrast, rises in sea level will

FACTS and FIGURES

POPULATION CHANGES

The projected percentage change in working-age populations between 2005 and 2020 if there is no net migration:

Japan	-11.6
Italy	-7.0
Germany	-6.2
Canada	-0.8
UK	0.3
France	0.5
United State	5.9

International Migration Outlook, 2009

increase flooding in coastal areas, such as in Bangladesh. These changes are likely to lead to stronger pressure on people to migrate.

Refugees

The predicted disastrous effects of climate change, added to the frequent outbreak of wars across the globe, will probably force increasing numbers to flee as refugees. Climate change, conflict and forced migration are linked. For example, in Darfur, Sudan, rainfall has already been declining over the past half a century. The desert is spreading. Arab nomads have less grazing land for their animals, and African and Arab settled farmers have less land and water for their farms. The competition between these groups for ever-decreasing resources has fanned the flames of conflict, and pushed many to leave. The origins and destinations of refugees will shift, depending on where crises like these occur.

What can be done?

These challenges can be addressed. Measures could be adopted to reduce the effects of climate change in the worst-affected countries. Fairer trade between countries could allow people in poor countries to earn higher incomes for their produce so they do not feel the urge to leave. Economic policies, such as investing more in developing countries to create more jobs, could help to narrow the gap between the rich and the poor countries.

CASE STUDY

FAIR TRADE BENEFITS

Oliva and her husband Joseph live in Uganda. They have seven children and four orphaned relatives to feed as well as school fees to pay. Everyone has to work hard. The family owns an organic coffee farm in Uganda. Oliva is responsible for the day-to-day running of the farm and helps to organize her local coffee cooperative. Joseph helps out and also has a job as an accountant. The children all work on the farm, weeding and picking coffee, feeding farm animals and doing cooking and cleaning. Since the family are members of a fair-trade cooperative, they receive a fair price for their coffee, fixed for the season. This allows them to budget and plan ahead with a sense of security. People like Oliva and Joseph have no need to migrate.

Fairtrade Foundation, January 2007

Developed countries could change their immigration policies. Most of them need unskilled workers but try to bar them from entry. The workers still arrive but do so illegally. Some experts, for example, in the United Nations Development Programme (UNDP), advocate relaxing immigration controls and improving cooperation between home and host countries to regulate the flow of labour. They argue there should be more schemes for people to migrate for seasonal work, such as in tourism and agriculture, and low-skilled workers should receive visas where their labour is required. Once they arrive, governments should protect their human rights, giving them equal pay to local people for doing the same job, and decent working conditions.

Whether governments adopt these strategies or not, migration will continue as an integral element in our globalized world. People will always move to achieve a better life – and who can blame them?

Immigrants and their supporters demonstrate in New York in 2006 for the right to remain in the country. US states regularly bring in laws to try to restrict illegal immigration, yet the lure of a better life continues to draw in hopeful migrants.

Glossary

aid Food, shelter or money that is given to people in need, for example, after a war.

brain drain When skilled and educated people in developed countries migrate to work abroad.

brothel A house where people pay to have sex with prostitutes.

colonial To do with the period when some powerful countries, especially in Europe, ruled other lands.

colony A country that is ruled by another country.

Communist A system of government that existed in the Soviet Union and its Eastern European satellites, in which the government controlled the production of goods and the running of services.

contract labourer A worker who is taken on to do a particular job on a temporary basis.

demographic To do with the changing number of births and deaths over a period of time.

developed countries Countries with a relatively high income per person, where most people have a high standard of living. They include most European countries, the United States, Canada, Australia, New Zealand and Japan.

developing countries Countries with a relatively low income per person, where most people have a low standard of living. They include the countries of Africa, Asia (except Japan), Latin America and the Caribbean.

emigration Moving to another country in order to live there on a permanent basis.

ethnic group A group of people who share a culture, tradition, way of life and sometimes language.

fair trade A system in which companies deal directly with producers and fix a fair price for their produce over a period of time.

family reunion A form of migration that allows family members to join a migrant in another country.

formal sector The official part of the economy, in which people's jobs are recorded and they pay tax to the government.

globalization A process by which countries around the world have become increasingly linked to each other through the rapid growth of trade, communications and travel.

host country The country that migrants move to.

human trafficker A criminal who deceives people into leaving their own country.

immigrant A person who comes to live permanently in a foreign country.

informal economy Economic activity that is neither taxed nor monitored by the government.

irregular migrant A person who has entered a country in violation of its immigration controls.

labour migration Migrating for work.

Latin America The parts of the Americas south of the United States where Spanish and Portuguese are spoken.

net migration The number of migrants when emigrants are subtracted from immigrants. For example, if there are 200,000 immigrants and 100,000 emigrants, net migration is 100,000.

nomadic Moving from place to place in search of grazing land for animals.

occupation Moving into another country and taking control of it using military force.

people smuggler A person who arranges for people to travel illegally to another country.

pilgrim A person going on a journey for a religious reason.

private sector The part of the economy made up of businesses that aim to make a profit.

refugee A person who escapes to another country to seek refuge from war, natural disaster or unfair treatment.

refugee camp A camp built by governments or international organizations to shelter large numbers of refugees.

remittance A transfer of money by a migrant working abroad to his or her home country.

service sector The part of the economy that provides services rather than making goods – for example, banking, transport, schools and hospitals.

sponsor In the Gulf States, an employer who agrees to take on a foreign worker to do a specific job.

transit country A country that migrants enter on their way to another country.

visa A mark in a person's passport that gives him or her permission to enter a country.

World Bank An international organization that lends money to developing countries and gives advice on economic policy.

Further Information

Books

Current Controversies: Immigration by Debra A Miller (editor) (Greenhaven Press, 2010)

Immigration by Tom Lansford (Greenhaven Press, 2009)

In the News: Illegal Immigration and Amnesty: Open Borders and National Security by Janet Levy (Rosen Publishing, 2010)

Migration and Refugees by Cath Senker (Smart Apple Media, 2008)

Should Immigration Be Restricted? by John Meany (Heinemann, 2008)

Websites

www.iom.int/jahia/Jahia/about-migration/facts-and-figures/lang/en
This website gives facts and figures about migration.

www.migrationinformation.org
This website gives migration data from around the world.

www.oxfam.org.uk/education/resources/category.htm?41
This Oxfam site offers resources on refugees and asylum seekers.

pstalker.com/migration/
Stalker's Guide to International Migration is a guide to the history of migration, why and how people migrate and the impact of migration.

www.refugeesinternational.org
The website of Refugees International, a US organization that helps refugees. There are links to information about current refugee crises.

Index

Page numbers in **bold** refer to maps and photos.

abuse of migrant workers 18
Afghanistan and Afghans 18, 21
Africa and Africans 6, 10–15, **13**, 12, 26, 31, 38–39, **39**, 40, 41
Algeria and Algerians 18, 19, 36
Argentina and Argentinians 6, 28, 31
Asia and Asians 6, 18, 20–27, 31, 40
Asia-Pacific Region 20–27, 40
Australia 6, 15, 20–21, 24, 25, 37

Bangladesh 22, 27, 42
brain drains 14, **14–15**, 26, 33, 44
Brazil and Brazilians 28, 31
Burma and Burmese 21, 22, 23, **23**, 30

Canada 15, 24, 25, 26, 28, 31, 32, 33, 40, 41
Caribbean 28, 33
China and Chinese 12, 22, 23, 25
circular migration 28
climate change 40, 41–42
conflict 7, 10, 21, 42

Darfur conflict 12, 42
Democratic Republic of Congo (DRC) 10, **11**, 12
demographic trends 40–41
Dominican Republic 28–30, 33

Eastern Europe 34–35, 36, 38
economic migrants 6, 10, 12, 16, 22, 24, 25, 34, 35
Egypt 16, 18
Eritrea and Eritreans 12, 18
Ethiopia 12, 18
Europe and Europeans 6, 10, 12, 18, 25, **29**, 31, 34–39, **37**, 40

family reunion 24, 28, 35, 44
France 12, 18, 35, **35**, 36, 37, 41

Germany 8, 18, 35, 36, 41
globalization 6, 28, 43, 44
Gulf States 16, 18, 20, 24, **27**, **41**

home countries, effects of migration on 14–15, 19, 26–27, 33, 38
host countries, effects of migration on 8, 15, 19, 26, 27, 32, 38
human trafficking 8, 21, 30, 44

India and Indians 22, 25, 26, 27, **41**
Indonesia and Indonesians 18, 20, 22, 23
Iraq and Iraqis 16, 17–18, 19, 30
Iran 16, 18, 21, 26
Ireland 36, 38
irregular migrants 6, 23, 25, 31, 32, 36, 37, 38, 42
Israel 16, 17
Italy and Italians 12, 31, 33, 35, 36, 38, 41

Japan 12, 22, 23, 25, 31, 41
Jordan 16, 18, 19

Latin America and Latin Americans 6, 21, 28, **29**, 30, 33, 34, 36, 40, 44
Lesotho 14, 15
Libya 12, 18, 40

Malawi and Malawians 14, 15
Malaysia 8, 22, 23
marriage migration 20, 23
Mexico and Mexicans 8, 28, 30, **30–31**, 32, 33
Middle East and North Africa (MENA) 16–19, **17**, 31, 36
Morocco and Moroccans 18, 19, 36, **39**

New Zealand 6, 20, 21, 24, 25, 37
North America 6, 12, **33**

Pakistan 16, 21, 22, 26
Palestinians 16, 17
people smuggling 25, 45
Philippines and Filipinos 16, **19**, 20, 23, 25
Poland and Polish 8, 36, 38
Portugal and Portuguese 31, 36

Qatar 16, 19

refugees 7, 10, 15, 16, 17–18, 19, 20, 21, 26, 42, 45
remittances 14, 19, 33, **33**, 38
restrictions on immigration 8, 19, 25, 31, 38, 40
Romania 16, 36

Saudi Arabia 16, 18, 40
Senegal and Senegalese 12
Singapore 8, 20, 22, 26
skilled migrants 9, 12, 14, 20, 25, 26, 32, 34, 38
Somalia and Somalis 10, 12, 15
South Africa 11, 12, **14–15**, 15, 21
South Korea 20, 22, 23, 26
Spain 12, 31, 33, 34, 35, 36, 37, 38–39
sub-Saharan Africa 10–15
Syria 16, 18, 19

Taiwan 20, 22–23, 26
temporary workers 6
Thailand 16, 22, 23, **23**, 25
transit migration 18
Tunisia 18, 19
Turks 18, 36

United Arab Emirates (UAE) 16, 19, 40, **41**
United Kingdom (UK) 14, 15, 25, 34, 35, 36, 38, 41
United States 8, 15, 24, 25, 28, 30, **30–31**, 31, 32, 33, 40, 41
unskilled or low-skilled migrants 9, 20, 24, 25, 26, 32, 34, 38, 42

Vietnam 8, 23, 25

West Bank and Gaza Strip 16, 17

Zimbabwe and Zimbabweans 10, 12, 15